THE AFGHANISTAN WAR

Frontline Soldiers and Their Families

Sarah Levete

Gareth Stevens
PUBLISHING

Please visit our website, **www.garethstevens.com**. For a free color catalog of all our high-quality books, call toll free 1-800-542-2595 or fax 1-877-542-2596.

Library of Congress Cataloging-in-Publication Data
Levete, Sarah.
The Afghanistan War: frontline soldiers and their families / by Sarah Levete.
p. cm. — (Frontline families)
Includes index.
ISBN 978-1-4824-3049-3 (pbk.)
ISBN 978-1-4824-3052-3 (6 pack)
ISBN 978-1-4824-3050-9 (library binding)
1. Afghan War, 2001- — Juvenile literature. I. Levete, Sarah. II. Title.
DS371.3 L48 2016
958.104—d23

First Edition

Published in 2016 by
Gareth Stevens Publishing
111 East 14th Street, Suite 349
New York, NY 10003

© 2016 Gareth Stevens Publishing

Produced by Calcium
Editors for Calcium: Sarah Eason and Rachel Warren Chadd
Designers: Paul Myerscough and Jessica Moon
Picture researcher: Susannah Jayes

Picture credits: Cover: Shutterstock: Tracing Tea; Inside: Dreamstime: Edmund Crabb 21b; Shutterstock: Larry Bruce 10, Orhan Cam 45t, Nate Derrick 9b, 40, John Gomez 39, Rainer Lesniewski 7, Manamana 43c, Lizette Potgieter 20, Specnaz 5, Pal Teravagimov 23b, 44, Tracing Tea 1, 24, 30; Wikipedia Commons: 11, Air Force Medical Service 31, Sheila Devera/DVIDSHUB 16, Nasim Fekrat 23t, Keith D. Henning 9t, Imperial War Museums 26, ISAF Headquarters Public Affairs Office 28, 37b, Bram Souffreau 33, Robert Thivierge 36, UK Department for International Development (DFID) 29, UK Ministry of Defence 35, U.S. Agency for International Development (USAID) 41t, 42, 43t, U.S. Army 12, 15, 17t, U.S. Department of Defense 4, 13, 14, 18, 27, 32, 45c, U.S. Marine Corps 19, 38, U.S. Navy 17b, 22, 41b.

Printed in the United States of America
CPSIA compliance information: Batch #CS15GS: For further information contact Gareth Stevens, New York, New York at 1-800-542-2595.

CONTENTS

CHAPTER 1

THE AFGHANISTAN WAR

A ten-year-old child in Afghanistan will know nothing but war in his or her country. The current Afghanistan War is a conflict that has lasted more than a decade. Afghan people have grown up with war and fear as daily parts of their lives.

Far and Wide

Thousands of families in Afghanistan and around the world have suffered as a result of the war. Innocent children and families in Afghanistan have been killed or injured. The war has drawn in armies directly from the United States, the United Kingdom, and other countries allied to the North Atlantic Treaty Organization (NATO). Men and women fighting in the war have lost their lives or faced life-changing injuries during the conflict. The war has had a huge and long-lasting effect on the families of all those victims.

In this book, we look at the ways in which the war has changed the lives of the many families who have been affected by the conflict.

This boy cannot remember a time when his country was not at war.

Afghanistan is a poor country, even though it receives much international aid. In rural and urban areas, homes and hospitals have been reduced to rubble during the fierce battles waged in the country. How do you think parents bring up their children living in such a devastated community?

About Afghanistan

Afghanistan is made up of many different clans and ethnic groups, including the Pashtuns, Tajiks, Hazaras, Uzbeks, Turkmens, Aimaqs, and Nuristanis. The family structure is very important in Afghan life. The main religion in Afghanistan is Islam. Religion lies at the root of Afghan society, affecting almost every aspect of people's lives, from how they dress to how they educate their children. The Taliban, against whom the NATO troops have fought, hold extremist religious views that do not allow ordinary Afghan girls and women basic rights, such as the right to an education.

A TIMELINE OF THE AFGHANISTAN WAR

Afghanistan has a long and troubled history. Years of conflict have left the country in poverty, with different groups taking advantage of the Afghan people's desperation. This timeline shows the key events leading up to and during the war.

1953
September 7: Mohammad Daud Khan becomes prime minister. He establishes strong links with the communist Soviet Union and introduces social changes, including more freedom for women.

1973
July 17: Daud Khan overthrows King Mohammad Zahir, and Afghanistan becomes a republic.

1978
April 28: Communist groups overthrow Daud Khan's moderate government. Tribal groups begin to rebel against the rule.

1979
December 24: Soviet army invades to support the communist government. Rebellion spreads across Afghanistan.

1989
February 15: Soviet withdrawal, sparking more fighting between warlords and tribal leaders.

1996
September 27: Taliban (extremist Islamic group) takes control, mainly in the south, but fighting continues with Northern Alliance, an anti-Taliban group active in the north of the country.

2001
September 9: Terrorist group al-Qaeda kills Ahmad Shah Massoud, commander of the Northern Alliance.

September 11: al-Qaeda hijacks four planes in the United States, crashing two into the World Trade Center in New York City, one into the Pentagon, and one in a field in Pennsylvania.

October 7: US and UK forces bomb Taliban strongholds, and troops are sent to Afghanistan.

Afghanistan is a landlocked country, bordered by Pakistan, Iran, Tajikistan, Uzbekistan, and Turkmenistan. This map shows the 34 provinces that make up Afghanistan.

November 13: Northern Alliance takes control of the Afghan capital, Kabul.

December 5: Hamid Karzai appointed temporary leader of Afghanistan.

December 7: Taliban surrender Kandahar, the largest city in southern Afghanistan.

December 20: United Nations (UN) Security Council establishes the International Security Assistance Force (ISAF).

2003

August 11: NATO takes over ISAF operations in Afghanistan, leading to the involvement of 49 different countries in the conflict.

2004

October 9: Hamid Karzai is elected President of Afghanistan.

2006

UK and Canadian forces sent to areas in southern Afghanistan, strongholds of the Taliban.

2009

December 1: President Obama commits more troops to Afghanistan.

2010

November: NATO countries agree to hand over security to Afghan forces by the end of 2014.

2011

May 2: Osama bin Laden, leader of terrorist group al-Qaeda, found in Pakistan and killed.

June 22: President Obama announces the gradual withdrawal of US troops.

2013

June: Afghan National Security Forces take over from ISAF.

2014

May 27: President Obama announces withdrawal of US troops by the end of 2016. Unrest continues.

AFGHAN POWER PLAYERS

After the withdrawal of the Soviet army in 1989, corrupt warlords and tribal leaders fought over parts of Afghanistan. Afghans longed for stability and order in their lives. Some Afghans thought the Taliban would provide some security for their families and communities. However, the Taliban rule was brutal and ruthless.

The Taliban

This group emerged in the early 1990s, after the Soviets withdrew from Afghanistan. It began as a collection of religious students, many of whom were educated in madrassas—extremist religious schools in Pakistan, where they had fled after the Soviet invasion. The Taliban promote a view of Islam that, among its other rules, forbids girls over the age of eight from going to school, forces women to wear a full covering veil—called a burka—in public, and bans television, music, and movies. Punishments for breaking any laws are brutal, including executions and cutting off limbs.

Northern Alliance

An anti-Taliban group, the Northern Alliance, is made up of groups of rebels, many of whom had fought each other before the Taliban gained control.

New Armies

In 2002, Hamid Karzai announced the creation of a new Afghan National Army (ANA). Before this, law and order were kept by groups of armed men under the command of warlords. Today, Afghan soldiers are partly responsible for

Afghan soldiers took on an increasingly important role in keeping peace in their country when the last of the international troops left at the end of 2014.

keeping law and order in the country. Until 2014, they worked alongside troops from 49 other nations, making up ISAF. The majority of troops came from the United States and the United Kingdom. The international organization NATO led the ISAF troops.

Primary Source: What Does It Tell Us?

This is a photograph of an Afghan man in an area of Kandahar, a Taliban stronghold that is mountainous and difficult to access. This type of terrain has provided hiding places for the Taliban that are extremely difficult for the international forces to reach. How do you think terrain such as this has made fighting the war difficult for the mostly Western soldiers?

CHAPTER 2

WHY WAR?

The latest conflict in Afghanistan's troubled and war-torn history erupted in 2001. It was triggered by the attack known as "9/11," launched on the United States on September 11, 2001, by the al-Qaeda terrorist group. While the Taliban was in power in Afghanistan, they allowed al-Qaeda to train its recruits there. The Taliban refused to give up Osama bin Laden, leader of al-Qaeda. As a result, the United States attacked. The war started in order to destroy al-Qaeda groups who were responsible for terrorist attacks around the world.

9/11

One sunny morning in 2001, terrorists took control of four American airplanes carrying civilians. They flew two of the planes directly into the World Trade Center (known as the Twin Towers) in New York City, home to thousands of workers. The buildings were completely

The United States wanted to take revenge on al-Qaeda for the attack on its country and people.

destroyed, with huge loss of life. Another plane was hijacked and crashed into the Pentagon. Yet another plane, destined for Washington, D.C., crashed into a field in Pennsylvania. A total of 2,997 people died in these attacks.

Understanding the War

Nearly 50 countries sent men and women from their armies to take part in the military action in a country far away from their homes. The first justification for the war on Afghanistan was to get rid of al-Qaeda terrorists to make the world a safer place. Within a few years, the reason for the military presence and action in Afghanistan had changed to meet the need to rebuild the shattered country and prevent the return of the Taliban. It was sometimes difficult for the families of those men and women who were in Afghanistan to understand why they were risking their lives in a distant country.

Primary Source: What Does It Tell Us?

This photograph shows the attack on the Twin Towers, which left thousands of families mourning the loss of a relative. The loss affected many children—1,300 children were orphaned and 17 babies were born to women who had lost their partner in the attacks. There was a huge increase in the number of people suffering from post-traumatic stress disorder (PTSD). How do you think those who witnessed the devastating attack on the Twin Towers and who suffered loss felt about the United States going to war in Afghanistan?

GOING TO WAR

The start of the Afghanistan War saw tearful farewells in many American families. Children hugged their mother or father goodbye, hoping to see them soon. The men and women did not know how brutal the war would turn out to be, or how long they would serve in Afghanistan.

A Question of Money

Sending troops thousands of miles away is a large and costly undertaking. While troops were in Afghanistan, the United States and the United Kingdom were about to embark on another war–in Iraq. Resources and funding for two wars stretches a country to the limit. Countries promised financial and other support for Afghanistan, but large amounts of this were wasted amid confusion about who took responsibility for funded projects.

Primary Source: What Does It Tell Us?

A key problem for the NATO forces in Afghanistan was the language barrier. Very few of the military were able to speak the native languages. How could the armies win the hearts and confidence of local people without being able to speak to them? The local translators, such as the man shown holding the information leaflet in this photograph, were a lifeline for the armies, although they put their lives at risk by doing their jobs. Why do you think being able to win the confidence of local people was so important to the war effort?

These US soldiers help an Afghan family carry tents that will provide the family with shelter after severe flooding.

Return of the Taliban

At first, it seemed as if the war had succeeded. However, Hamid Karzai's government was weak and corrupt. There were many unsuccessful attempts on his life. By the beginning of 2005, the Taliban were regrouping and were back on the attack. The focus for many of the international soldiers was now to protect the local people from the Taliban insurgents, rather than focusing on rebuilding the country.

Although the US and NATO forces had vast amounts of equipment, from tanks to bomber planes, they did not have the knowledge of the local area or people that the Taliban had. In 2006, United Kingdom and Canadian troops were sent to the most troubled areas in Afghanistan. There, they suffered their greatest losses. Families at home began to wonder how long the war would continue without obvious success.

FAMILY LOYALTY

Some Afghans viewed the international forces as enemy occupiers. Others welcomed the forces as peacemakers who would make their world safer and better. Afghan families were torn apart. Some men decided to fight for the Taliban, sometimes joining the insurgents in revenge for the death or wounding of a relative caught up in the cross fire. Others decided to join the Afghan police or army and work alongside NATO forces.

Training Young Children

Many poor families were persuaded to send their young boys to madrassas (where they received a free education) in Pakistan. However, some of the madrassas trained the children to fight in a holy war, or jihad. Some of these children were trained as suicide bombers.

The family structure is very important in Afghan culture. However, opposing views about the war caused huge rifts and often split family loyalties.

Families sent their children to madrassas in the belief that doing so would improve their lives. However, in many instances it meant their children came to believe in an extreme version of Islam that required them to sacrifice their lives.

Afghan Army

For any Afghan, joining the Afghan army was a bold and brave decision. As the US and UK forces named the time of their eventual withdrawal from Afghanistan, they knew they had to prepare the Afghan army to take their place and continue to protect areas from the advances of the Taliban. There were tempting rewards for Afghan men who joined the army. Recruits received a larger than average salary and were given regular lessons in reading and writing. They had to agree to serve for at least five years, but at the end of this time recruits would have been taught basic literacy skills that most Afghans lacked—skills that would improve their prospects.

Primary Source: What Does It Tell Us?

This photograph from 2007 shows an ANA soldier engaged in a firefight with extremists in Helmand Province in southern Afghanistan. Brothers and friends were divided over their support for one side or the other. How do you think this affected the family structure in Afghanistan?

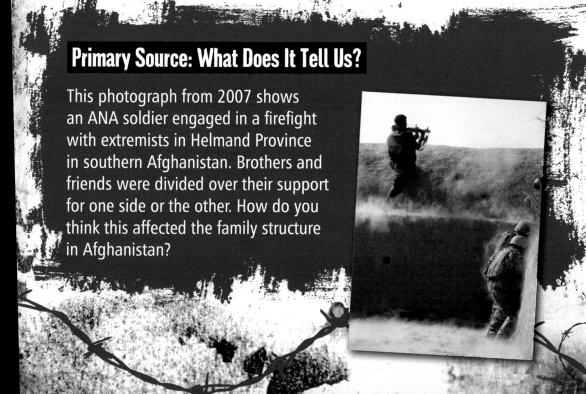

At first, many Afghans welcomed the ISAF. It arrived with the promise of security and safety for families who had long suffered under the brutal Taliban regime. Afghans hoped the forces would help them rebuild their country so that families could live easier and more prosperous lives. ISAF forces needed the support of ordinary Afghans to help them prevent a return of the Taliban rule.

Winning Trust

The US government airdropped thousands of aid packets for displaced Afghans who had been forced to leave their homes. Each packet contained enough nutrients and calories for one person for one day. The US and NATO forces hoped such actions would persuade the Afghan people to trust them.

Propaganda

As the war continued, many Afghans became impatient with the slow pace of progress in their country's development. They became angered by the corruption of local leaders and the government. Such views made it much easier for the Taliban to move into communities. The Taliban used social media such as Facebook and Twitter to try to spread the word about the evils of the invading armies.

Army doctors helped save this child, who was wounded when his family's home was damaged in a gas explosion.

Primary Source: What Does It Tell Us?

The writing on this leaflet, in the Pashto language, reads:

Children need a peaceful, hopeful, and happy life.
Help us in making Afghanistan happy again,
Whether you want a life like this for your women and children.

The US army airdropped propaganda leaflets such as these to try to build links with the local Afghan people. It wanted and needed ordinary Afghan families on its side if it were to win the war against the Taliban. Do you think doing this would have the effect of encouraging a family to support the international troops?

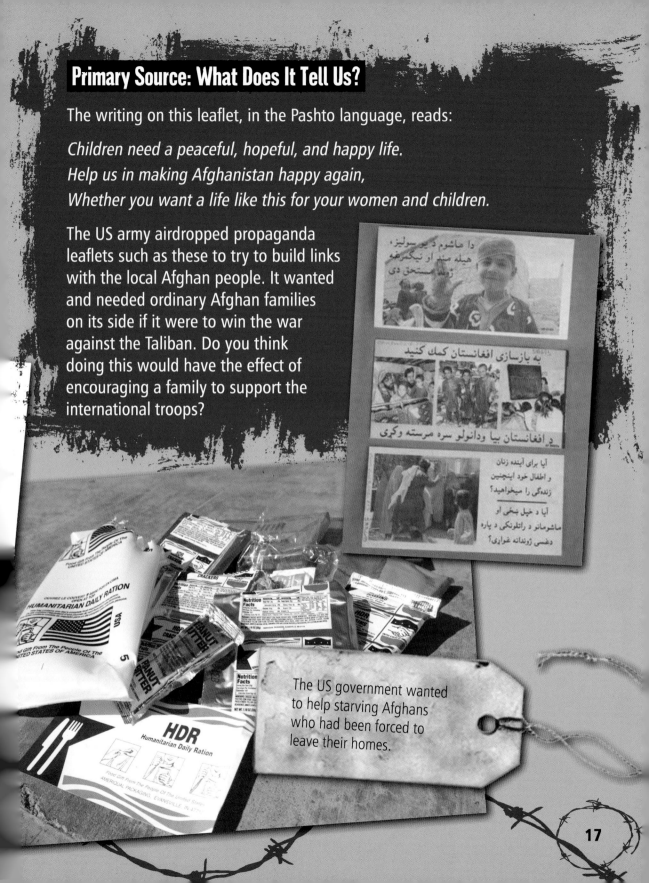

The US government wanted to help starving Afghans who had been forced to leave their homes.

Afghans had longed for peace and help to build up their country. However, progress was slow. Dropping bombs from the air may have helped repel the Taliban, but it also destroyed villages and killed and injured innocent Afghans. ISAF forces became less popular with the Afghan people.

Innocent Deaths

NATO and US forces used air strikes to attack Taliban fighters, but the insurgents often hid in villages, where ordinary families lived. Many innocent victims were killed in such air strikes. In one tragedy, the Taliban fired a rocket at a US base. A US plane then dropped two bombs onto a house where the Taliban had been seen to go. A family home was blown up and nine civilians were reported dead. In another tragedy, a family traveling to a wedding were all killed when an air strike hit the party. The bride was among the dead.

Primary Source: What Does It Tell Us?

The Afghan soldiers in this photograph are searching Afghan men. This had been part of daily life since the start of the war. How do you think children felt when their relatives were always suspected of carrying a bomb or weapon?

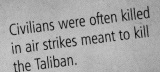
Civilians were often killed in air strikes meant to kill the Taliban.

Human Shields

The Taliban used women and children as "human shields." They lined up women and children on a roof and fired at enemy troops from behind them. If the opposition did not fight back, they risked their own lives. If they did fire back, they risked killing innocent people. The Taliban knew how damaging it was for ISAF when they mistakenly killed civilians.

Losing Hope

In 2005, when the Taliban recovered as a fighting force, many Afghans despaired. If the war had been to rid them of the Taliban, why were they able to return? Afghans could see no reason then for the tragedies that had befallen many innocent families.

Insults Against Afghans

Reports of Afghan prisoners being abused and hurt in prisons run by the US military further inflamed public opinion and pushed some Afghans toward the Taliban. Soldiers on the largest US base, in Bagram, burned copies of the Koran, the holy book of Islam. They were possibly unaware of the insult this caused and of the sacred nature of the text. This sparked off riots and killings of Afghan and NATO soldiers.

CHAPTER 3

LIVING THROUGH THE WAR

There are no exact figures for the number of civilian deaths in Afghanistan, but estimates suggest it could be as much as a shocking 21,000. That means 21,000 families grieving. This figure does not include the many men, women, and children injured physically or mentally as a result of the war.

No Systems

Before the war, Afghanistan was already suffering because of poverty, particularly in rural and isolated areas. Earthquakes often rock the country, killing people and destroying homes and buildings. Years of turmoil had left the government disorganized. There were few effective systems in place to support essentials such as health care and road networks. Troops were used to help create better ways to support these essential facilities that would make life easier for families in Afghanistan.

This Afghan mother, her face covered by a burka, risks her own safety by seeking medical help for her child.

A Man's World

The extreme beliefs of the Taliban meant that women in Afghanistan had very little freedom and hardly any rights. One of the goals of the NATO intervention was to improve the lives of women and children.

No Safety at Home

Home is meant to be a place of safety across the world. NATO forces often raided homes at night, to try to find the Taliban. This caused huge stress for families and further weakened the trust between some ordinary Afghans and the international soldiers.

Innocent men, women, and children were as much at risk from hidden bombs as the troops they were intended for.

Primary Source: What Does It Tell Us?

Soldiers from international armies came to Afghanistan. Foreign soldiers used translators to help them talk to local people. This often placed the translators at great risk of attack on themselves or their families by the Taliban. Do you think Afghan families would feel reassured or threatened by having foreign troops in their country? How do you think families felt to be under the control of foreign soldiers such as this American, who could not speak their language?

LIFE FOR WOMEN

Defeating the Taliban has to some extent improved the terrible conditions under which Afghan girls and women live. Afghanistan had long had strict traditions about the role of women in society. It was only in 1959 that the Afghan government passed laws to allow women a choice about wearing a veil. Under the Taliban, women were forbidden from showing any flesh in public, and the punishments for doing so were severe.

Hidden Women

Before the US-led intervention, women were confined to their homes unless with a male. They had to live behind darkened windows so that men (other than their husbands) could not see their faces. They were forced to wear a full body veil. They were not allowed to work or to get health care from any men—and with women not allowed to work it was almost impossible for them to receive professional health care.

Women and girls who disobeyed rules faced brutal punishments. Young Afghan girls were often forced into marriage or even sold. Afghanistan is a very male-dominated society and there was little justice for women. The international troops wanted to improve the repressed existence of women under the Taliban rule.

In 2010, these women were training to become police officers. This would have been unthinkable under Taliban rule.

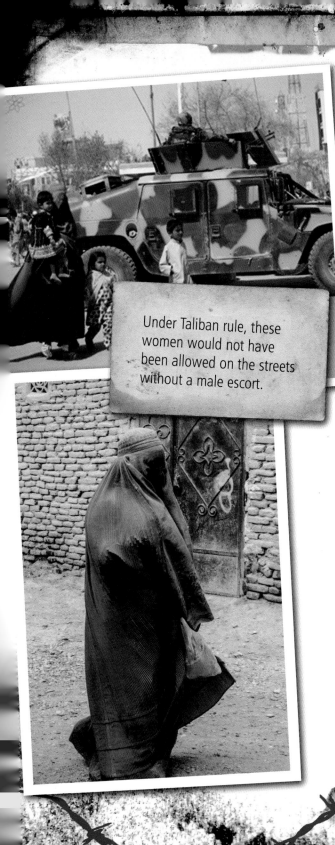

Under Taliban rule, these women would not have been allowed on the streets without a male escort.

New Hopes, New Challenges

Today, there are many women active in the Afghan government. Women have more freedom, and there are opportunities for girls to go to school beyond the age of eight—something that was forbidden by the Taliban. These new freedoms are more common in urban areas, but women in remote villages are less likely to benefit from such changes. As women find the confidence and security to work, learn, and have a voice in the running of the country, they again become targets of the insurgent Taliban.

Returning Dangers

In 2003, women's rights became part of Afghan law. However, since the gradual withdrawal of international troops, and with the Taliban still in control of parts of the country, women once again suffer. According to an international poll, conducted in 2011, Afghanistan is the most dangerous country in the world to live in as a woman.

LIFE FOR CHILDREN

Growing up in Afghanistan today means growing up in a violent world. That is all that many children have ever known. According to Daniel Toole, UNICEF Director for South Asia, "Afghanistan is the most difficult place to be born as a child."

Dying Young

Children have suffered hugely in the war. According to a 2013 report by the United Nations, 1,304 Afghan children were killed or injured in violence due to the war in 2012. Of that number, 399 casualties were caused by "improvised explosive devices" (IEDs) and 110 by suicide bombers, some of whom were children themselves.

Young and Homeless

Thousands of children have been separated from their parents or orphaned. Thousands of Afghans have been forced to flee their homes to find safer places to live. There are around half a million "internally displaced people" in Afghanistan—people who have been forced to move to a safer place within their country. Almost half of them are under 18 years old.

These children have known only poverty and hardship in their young lives.

These girls live in one of the most dangerous places in Afghanistan—Helmand Province. They are caught between the UK and US troops trying to protect them and the Taliban fighters. How do you think their experiences will shape their lives as adults?

The eggs that this young girl was selling have been smashed, possibly by Taliban members. The troops might be providing safety and support, but their efforts have not helped this little girl.

No Food

With Afghanistan's economy in ruins, there is little or no money to support children and families who cannot afford to feed themselves. It is estimated that one in every three children in Afghanistan under the age of five is moderately or severely underweight because they do not get enough to eat. Young children are often forced to work on the streets to earn money so they can eat.

Education for Children

The Soviet invasion, the civil war, and the extreme Taliban regime destroyed Afghanistan's education system. Under the Taliban, girls over eight were not allowed to go to school, and there was little opportunity for boys. As a result, more than half the population is illiterate, which means they cannot read or write.

CHAPTER 4

A WORLD OF FEAR

The Afghan conflict has spared no one. People of all nationalities working for the military or for charitable organizations, as well as civilians, have been at risk. No one was safe in the war and everyone was afraid. This fear continues to haunt those in Afghanistan today.

A Dangerous Place

Afghanistan is still a dangerous place. Families going to a market to buy some food risk attack from a suicide bomber, aimed at foreigners or troops. Children playing in a road risk harm from IEDs. The Taliban could be anywhere–hidden in markets, hidden in homes. As troops try to unearth the Taliban, innocent civilians often get hurt.

No Safety

"Green" is the US army's slang for Afghan or "host nation" armed forces.

This child has been injured by a bomb while traveling along the main road through Helmand Province. The young child and other injured were airlifted by helicopter to Camp Bastion, the UK military base in Helmand Province, for emergency medical treatment.

A child is talking to a US soldier in the province of Kandahar. How do you think the boy feels? Is he reassured by the soldier's presence, or does he consider him an enemy?

There have been many times when local troops opened fire on their own colleagues—these attacks are known as "green on green." The name given to incidents where Afghan security forces turn their guns on their NATO counterparts is "green on blue." This has led to huge distrust and fear among the NATO troops and their Afghan colleagues.

Troops have lived in fear. They do not know who to trust. Suicide bombers cruelly take advantage of the goodwill of the men and women. For example, a man deliberately injured his leg and went to seek medical assistance from UK soldiers. As they treated the man, he set off a bomb attached to his body, killing both himself and the soldiers.

Drone Attack

The US and UK armies have used drones in Afghanistan. These are unmanned flights, controlled from the ground. A study has shown that they cause ten times more casualties than conventional planes.

The war in Afghanistan has been devastating for children, with millions orphaned or sometimes just abandoned. These children will have to live with the memory of the traumatic experience of dodging bombs, being suspicious of everyone, and constant danger.

Mental Injury

Living under a bombardment of bombs, gunfire, and fear can cause long-term mental health problems. These are invisible injuries that cannot be mended by a quick visit to the hospital. Moreover, in Afghanistan there is little support for the men, women, and children who have suffered emotional trauma from the war.

Orphaned Children

Thousands of children in Afghanistan have been orphaned during this most recent conflict. The Taliban often try to recruit these young and vulnerable children. Some children find safety and friendship at an orphanage.

The children at this orphanage in Kabul have been given clothing. Workers at the orphanage hope to educate the children so that they can make their own informed choices about whom to support and how to live.

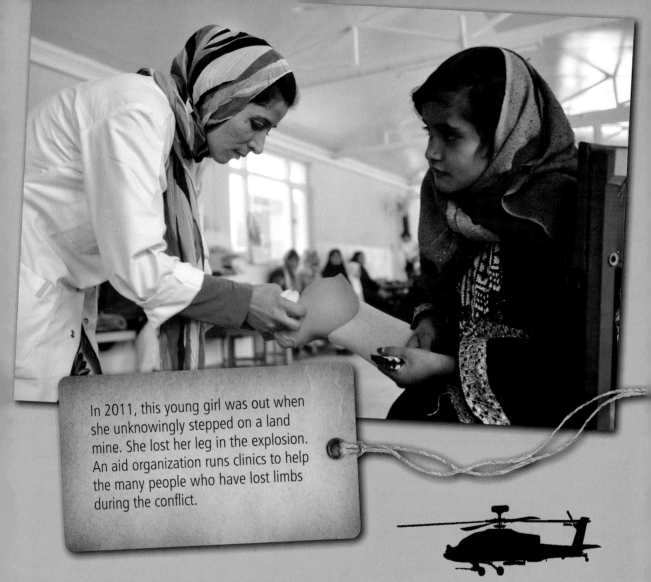

In 2011, this young girl was out when she unknowingly stepped on a land mine. She lost her leg in the explosion. An aid organization runs clinics to help the many people who have lost limbs during the conflict.

Widows in Afghanistan

The United Nations estimates that decades of wars in Afghanistan have left about 2 million women as widows. Some of these will have been widowed during the Soviet invasion and then the civil war that followed. Others will have lost their husbands during the most recent war. Afghanistan is a male-dominated society. Many widows lost their freedom to go out and socialize, and many lost their role in their community.

TRYING TO HELP

Rebuilding Afghanistan has involved the military, international charities, and aid organizations. For every volunteer or person helping in Afghanistan, there is a family worrying about the safety and well-being of a loved one. Even with the presence of soldiers and better-trained Afghan security forces, Afghanistan remains to this day a dangerous place in which to work and live.

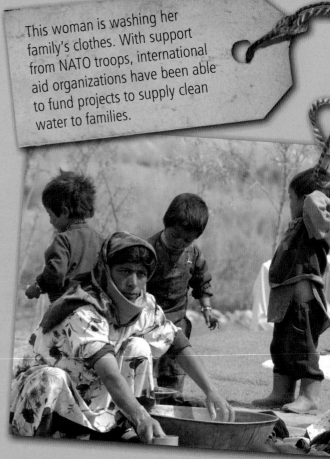

This woman is washing her family's clothes. With support from NATO troops, international aid organizations have been able to fund projects to supply clean water to families.

Danger for Foreigners

Without journalists and reporters, people around the world would know little about the Afghanistan conflict. Journalists keep the public informed about events happening far away. However, as they do so, they face real danger. The Taliban target any foreigners, whether or not they are working for the military. Since the start of the conflict in 2001, more than 40 journalists have been killed or kidnapped.

Injured Kathleen Kenna is transferred from a US airplane to a hospital in March 2002. Kenna, a 47-year-old reporter for the *Toronto Star* newspaper, had gone on an assignment to Afghanistan to report on the war. As she was traveling along a road, a grenade was thrown into the car, exploding under her seat. Kenna survived the attack but was seriously wounded.

Earlier that day, Kenna had witnessed US air strikes. Kenna thinks that the men who threw the grenade may not have distinguished between a foreign reporter and a foreign soldier. Do you think it is important that journalists visit war zones to report back, despite the dangers?

Killing Aid Workers

In 2014, an English aid advisor named Del Singh was dining out in a restaurant in the capital, Kabul. Terrorists attacked the restaurant, killing 21 people, including Del Singh. The restaurant had been heavily guarded, but a suicide bomber blew up the steel gates outside the restaurant and two gunmen then opened fire on diners and staff. Del Singh was in Afghanistan to make sure that money for aid was being spent correctly and most effectively for those families most in need. Back in England, his partner and sisters were devastated by the loss of their loved family member.

MADE HOMELESS BY WAR

At some point in their lives, one in four of Afghanistan's more than 30 million citizens is or has been a refugee. The years of war, unrest, and invasion have forced families to break up and some relatives to flee to other countries.

A Country of Refugees

The Soviet invasion in 1979 and subsequent occupation triggered waves of people seeking refuge in other parts of Afghanistan, as well as in other countries. An estimated 6 million Afghans left their homes and moved across the borders, including 3.5 million to Pakistan. Afghans fled again under the Taliban. Increasingly, millions of displaced Afghans have had to leave their homes to find a safer place in their own country.

This little boy lives in a refugee camp in Kabul. For him, it is the only home he knows.

Leaving and Returning Home

When the Soviets left Afghanistan, many Afghans who had supported the Soviets also left. Many refugees who had gone to Pakistan returned to their homeland. After the civil war, when the Taliban took control, many women left the country to escape the extreme rules of the Taliban movement.

The war has caused much migration from cities to rural areas. People wanted to move their families to a safer area, to escape US and NATO bombing that was often focused on urban areas. Many wanted also to avoid being forced into supporting the Taliban.

Primary Source: What Does It Tell Us?

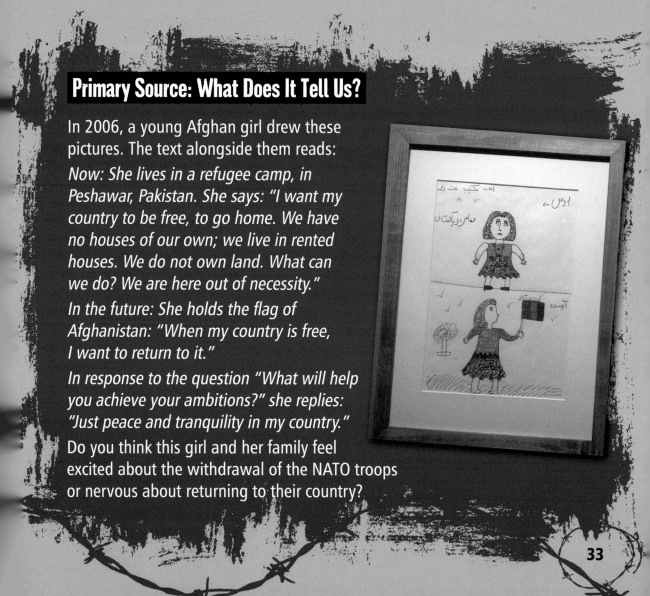

In 2006, a young Afghan girl drew these pictures. The text alongside them reads:

Now: She lives in a refugee camp, in Peshawar, Pakistan. She says: "I want my country to be free, to go home. We have no houses of our own; we live in rented houses. We do not own land. What can we do? We are here out of necessity."

In the future: She holds the flag of Afghanistan: "When my country is free, I want to return to it."

In response to the question "What will help you achieve your ambitions?" she replies: "Just peace and tranquility in my country."

Do you think this girl and her family feel excited about the withdrawal of the NATO troops or nervous about returning to their country?

CHAPTER 5

HOME AND AWAY

By 2011, there were approximately 140,000 US and other NATO troops in Afghanistan. Thousands of these troops were women, working in both combat and support roles. While the Afghan people and their families suffered, so too did the men and women sent to Afghanistan to prevent the rise of the Taliban and to help rebuild the country. For every soldier or aid worker killed, somewhere a family grieved.

Countless Loses

By the end of 2014, 453 UK troops and 2,356 US troops had been killed. That is more than 2,800 families mourning the loss of a relative. These numbers do not take into account the further thousands of men and women injured or struck down by disease.

Fear and Worry

For a UK soldier, the average tour of duty in Afghanistan was 6-12 months. For US soldiers, it was 15 months. During this time, families at home tried to continue with their lives as usual, despite the constant anxiety about a relative's safety and well-being. Detailed news reports in all media were a constant reminder of the danger the men and women faced. Children missed a parent and worried for his or her safety.

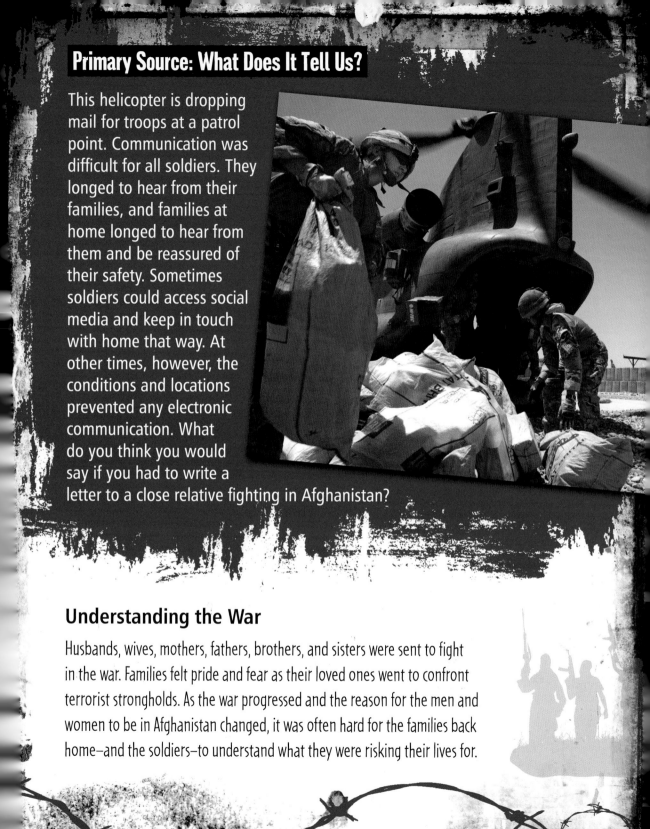

Primary Source: What Does It Tell Us?

This helicopter is dropping mail for troops at a patrol point. Communication was difficult for all soldiers. They longed to hear from their families, and families at home longed to hear from them and be reassured of their safety. Sometimes soldiers could access social media and keep in touch with home that way. At other times, however, the conditions and locations prevented any electronic communication. What do you think you would say if you had to write a letter to a close relative fighting in Afghanistan?

Understanding the War

Husbands, wives, mothers, fathers, brothers, and sisters were sent to fight in the war. Families felt pride and fear as their loved ones went to confront terrorist strongholds. As the war progressed and the reason for the men and women to be in Afghanistan changed, it was often hard for the families back home—and the soldiers—to understand what they were risking their lives for.

While soldiers from many countries were serving in Afghanistan, there was growing disquiet back home. At the start of the war, public opinion was generally in favor of the use of troops to get rid of the Taliban and al-Qaeda groups. However, as the war continued and more and more troops lost their lives or were injured, public opinion changed.

Losing Support

The war had become about rebuilding Afghanistan, but the troops were still at risk. The public could not see an end to the casualties or significant change in Afghanistan. Polls in both the United States and United Kingdom (the countries providing the largest number of troops) showed a decline in public support for the war.

Primary Source: What Does It Tell Us?

These people are protesting against the war. Many people were angered by the number of innocent Afghans killed in military attacks and did not want their home country to continue support for the war. What effect do you think this had on families whose loved ones were serving in the war, or who had lost a family member?

The heavy loss of soldiers in Afghanistan had a huge impact on public feeling as families mourned loved ones who would never return from the war.

People who had lost someone close to them in the war found it hard to accept that the lives of soldiers were still being put in danger and money was still being invested in unknown people in a country far away.

Failing the Troops

Families of soldiers were dismayed by reports from relatives that there was a lack of suitable equipment. This placed the troops in greater danger. An investigation into the death of one soldier who was shot by the Taliban highlighted the poor equipment the soldier had been using. Families were distraught that deaths might have been avoided.

NEW BATTLES TO FIGHT

Every family with a relative in Afghanistan dreaded a knock at the door or a telephone call that might bring terrible news. Thousands of soldiers lost their lives, and thousands more have suffered often life-changing physical injuries or mental health problems. For every soldier's death, injury, or mental damage, a family has also suffered.

Severe Injuries

Soldiers have returned from the war with terrible injuries. Some had limbs amputated, others had been badly burned in explosions or suffered severe brain injuries. For these men and women and their families, life would never be the same again. Many returning soldiers were disabled for life and would have to adapt to completely new circumstances.

Severe Stress

A sudden loud noise or just a banging door can trigger overwhelming fear and alarm in someone suffering from PTSD. The sufferers experience nightmares and

This soldier lost his leg when an IED exploded beneath him when he was on patrol in Afghanistan. Since then, he has become an army trainer and is here shown balancing a rifle on his artificial leg.

flashbacks, and may find it difficult to connect with their families, causing upset and hurt for loved ones. Often, PTSD is so severe that the returning soldiers are unable to find work, hold down a job, or maintain relationships. These invisible mental injuries are a result of troops seeing friends and colleagues dying from terrible injuries or witnessing the suffering the violence caused.

Families longed for the return of a relative. They hoped to resume family life as it had been before the war. However, men and women suffering from PTSD are often withdrawn, moody, and unpredictable. This has had a damaging effect on their partners and children.

Increasing numbers of war veterans need help for the trauma caused by the war.

CHAPTER 6

FUTURE FAMILIES

Since 2010, there has been a gradual withdrawal of troops from Afghanistan. Where does this leave the Afghan people? How does this affect the men and women who served in Afghanistan or the families of those men and women who died during the war?

Can Afghanistan Change?

Afghanistan was a poor and weak country before the most recent war. As the last troops withdraw from the country, Afghanistan is still poor and weak, although there have been considerable changes in the society. Only time will demonstrate the permanence of these positive changes.

These Afghans are making repairs to a building. A lot of time and money will need to be invested in the country to make life there better for ordinary people.

In Helmand, there are improved roads, and the area is generally safer. Women, particularly in large towns and cities, have more freedom. Education is improved, particularly for girls. However, the Taliban, against whom the war was fought, are still a dangerous presence in Afghanistan.

Primary Source: What Does It Tell Us?

A program set up by the US Army enabled these women to study to become midwives. With their new skills, they could return to their villages and help save the lives of women in childbirth. Think about the other changes in Afghan society that can be achieved with women able to work. How do you think this will have an effect on Afghanistan in the future?

Under Taliban rule, these girls faced a future of restrictions and fear. They have only ever experienced a country at war. Today, there are now more schools and educational opportunities for girls in Afghanistan.

New Dangers

Since the gradual withdrawal of the international armies, there has been an increase in attacks on innocent civilians and foreign workers. In 2014, a South African father running an education charity was killed in a Taliban attack in Kabul, along with his two teenage children—a son of 17 and a daughter of 15. When the attack happened, the children's mother was returning home from a clinic in Kabul where she worked.

SUPPORTING CHANGE

Afghanistan is a poor country. It will need continued financial support to keep in place the advances achieved by the war, particularly in education and health care.

Returning Home

Almost 6 million refugees have returned home since the Taliban were initially defeated. About 600,000 Afghans are still recognized as internally displaced. All of these people will need continued support to help them rebuild their lives and prepare for a future with their families.

Learning to Learn

In 2001, no girls attended formal schools, and there were only 1 million boys enrolled. By 2012, according to the World Bank, 7.8 million pupils attended school, and 2.9 million of those pupils were girls. More women are now able to read and write, skills that will enable them to work and to help provide for their families.

Many schools are still basic, sometimes based in tents or simply under trees. It will take money to improve and increase the number of schools and to train more teachers.

Advances in health care promise a better future for Afghan children.

In 2004, this truck traveled from Pakistan to Afghanistan, carrying many refugees who had fled Taliban rule. How do you think the families felt when they first returned to their villages? What challenges and opportunities do you think these families face now the war has come to an end and the international troops leave?

Drug Trade

Afghanistan is the world's largest supplier of poppies, the raw material used to make the drug heroin. This addictive drug is sold around the world, making huge amounts of money for the people who provide it. One goal of the military action in Afghanistan was to encourage farmers to grow alternative crops and halt the supply of poppies for making drugs.

Supported by ISAF, farmers were offered seeds to grow wheat and cotton and given support to switch to different crops. In a number of areas, this was successful, but some farmers moved elsewhere to grow poppies, with protection from the Taliban, who take large profits from the industry. Farmers make more money from the sale of poppies than they do from other crops.

Poppy growing in Afghanistan has increased since the start of the war.

THE LEGACY OF AFGHANISTAN

At the time of writing, the majority of troops have withdrawn from Afghanistan. Afghans have been able to vote in elections. At the cost of thousands of lives in this long war, there are significant improvements in society, especially for women. Girls are able to attend school, and there is better education available. Health care has improved.

However, the Taliban are still attacking foreigners and punishing Afghans who do not live by their strict command. Larger towns and cities are more likely to have benefited from the positive changes than rural areas, which still suffer from extreme poverty and hardship.

Soccer Again

Once, the soccer stadium in Kabul was a blood-soaked field, where the Taliban performed public executions. Today, a women's soccer team plays there with enthusiasm and freedom. If the Taliban return to power, this would be unthinkable.

Families in Afghanistan hope that one day their country will become a safe and bustling place, where girls and boys can look forward to a good future.

Primary Source: What Does It Tell Us?

There have been advances in Afghanistan—but there have also been setbacks. How do you think families and friends feel about the war as they lay flowers by the headstones of loved ones lost during the war?

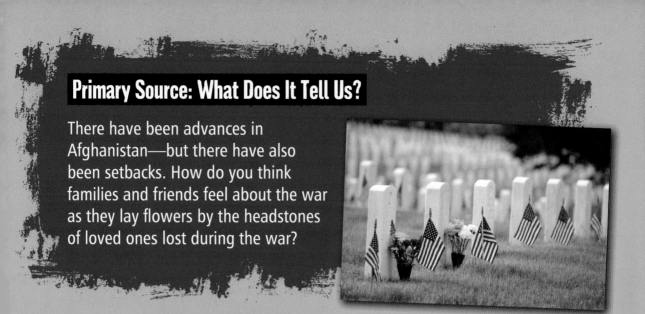

One day, Afghans hope their country will be free of war and terror, so that people can live without fear.

Support for Victims

With no systems in place to offer support to war victims in Afghanistan, people suffer terrible physical and emotional difficulties. Substantial investment into the country's economy will be needed to help heal the effects of war and build a new future for the Afghan people.

War or Peace?

Years of conflict have created a unique tradition. Weavers in Afghanistan made rugs that depicted images of the war. When the Soviet tanks invaded in 1979, Afghan weavers showed tanks and weapons. More recently, rugs have been woven with images of bombs and soldiers. The hope for Afghan families is that rugs will soon only show images of peace and prosperity.

GLOSSARY

burka full body and face covering

clan group based on local or family ties

communist person who believes in creating an equal society through government control of property and many other areas of life

economy country's money and finances

ethnic based on cultural traditions and religious beliefs

insurgents people who fight their government or an invading army

internally displaced forced to move from one part of a country to another

International Security Assistance Force (ISAF) military force set up by the United Nations to help protect and rebuild Afghanistan

intervention action to solve a problem

Islam the religion of Muslims

jihad "holy" war

migration movement of people from one country to another

North Atlantic Treaty Organisation (NATO) international organization that brings together the armies of different member countries

post-traumatic stress disorder (PTSD) mental condition that affects people who have had a shocking experience

propaganda information that tries to persuade people to believe one particular point of view

refugee person who has to leave their home or country for their own safety

repressed not free to do as a person wishes

Soviet Union communist state that existed from 1922 to 1991, made up of different countries, including Russia

stronghold place dominated by people who hold a particular belief, and where they protect themselves from attack

suicide bombers people who deliberately kill themselves to cause death and destruction

terrorist person who uses violence to force a government to change

tribal having strong links to local clans

UNICEF UN organization that looks after the interests of children around the world

United Nations (UN) organization that promotes international cooperation

warlords leaders of small communities who rule through fear

FOR MORE INFORMATION

Books

Doeden, Matt, and Blake Hoena. *War in Afghanistan: An Interactive Modern History Adventure* (You Choose: Modern History). North Mankato, MN: Capstone Press, 2014.

Winter, Max. *The Afghanistan War* (Wars in US History). North Mankato, MN: Child's World, 2015.

Zeiger, Jennifer. *The War in Afghanistan* (Cornerstones of Freedom: Third). New York, NY: Scholastic. 2011.

Websites

Find out more about Afghanistan at:
www.afghan-web.com

Learn more about the history of the war at:
www.cfr.org/afghanistan/us-war-afghanistan/p20018

Discover more about Afghanistan and its history at:
www.ducksters.com/geography/country/afghanistan.php

INDEX